First World War
and Army of Occupation
War Diary
France, Belgium and Germany

4 CAVALRY DIVISION
Divisional Troops
Jodhpur Imperial Service Lancers
1 January 1917 - 28 February 1918

WO95/1158/1

The Naval & Military Press Ltd
www.nmarchive.com
Published in association with The National Archives

Published by

The Naval & Military Press Ltd

Unit 10 Ridgewood Industrial Park,

Uckfield, East Sussex,

TN22 5QE England

Tel: +44 (0) 1825 749494

www.naval-military-press.com

www.nmarchive.com

This diary has been reprinted in facsimile from the original. Any imperfections are inevitably reproduced and the quality may fall short of modern type and cartographic standards.

© **Crown Copyright**
Images reproduced by permission of The National Archives, London, England, 2015.

Contents

Document type	Place/Title	Date From	Date To
Heading	WO95/1158/1		
Heading	1917-1918 4th Cavalry Division (Attd) Jodhpur Imp. Serv. Lancers Jan 1917 to Feb 1918 to Egypt L of C Palestine		
Heading	War Diary of Jodhpur Imperial Service Lancers From 1st January 1917 To 31st January 1917		
War Diary	Valines-St Marc-Saucourt-Franleu	01/01/1917	31/01/1917
Heading	Jodhpur Imperial Service Lancers 1st To 28th February 1917		
War Diary	Valines-Saucourt-Franleu-St Marc	15/02/1917	31/03/1917
Heading	War Diary of Jodhpur Lancers For The Month of April, 1917		
War Diary	Albert	01/04/1917	06/04/1917
War Diary	Bihucourt	07/04/1917	14/04/1917
War Diary	Bus-En-Artois	15/04/1917	30/04/1917
Heading	War Diary of Jodhpur Lancers For The Month of May, 1917-June 1917		
War Diary	Bus En Artois	01/05/1917	15/05/1917
War Diary	Meaulte	16/05/1917	16/05/1917
War Diary	Suzanne	17/05/1917	17/05/1917
War Diary	Mesnil Lebruntel	18/05/1917	24/05/1917
War Diary	Hamelet	25/05/1917	31/05/1917
Heading	War Diary of Jodhpur Lancers June, 1917		
War Diary	Camp Between Namelet And Roisel	01/06/1917	30/06/1917
Heading	War Diary of Jodhpur Lancers. For The Month of July, 1917		
War Diary	Hamelet	01/07/1917	05/07/1917
War Diary	Le Mesnil	06/07/1917	31/07/1917
Heading	War Diary of Jodhpur Lancers For August, 1917		
War Diary	Le Mesnil	01/08/1917	31/08/1917
Heading	War Diary of Jodhpur Lancers. For The Month of September, 1917		
War Diary	Le Mesnil	01/09/1917	30/09/1917
Heading	War Diary of Jodhpur Lancers. For The Month of October, 1917		
War Diary	Le Mesnil	01/10/1917	30/10/1917
War Diary	Devist	31/10/1917	31/10/1917
Heading	War Diary For November, 1917 Of The Jodhpur Lancers.		
War Diary	Devise	01/11/1917	15/11/1917
War Diary	Longasvenes	19/11/1917	19/11/1917
War Diary	Levacquerie	20/11/1917	20/11/1917
War Diary	Fins	21/11/1917	22/11/1917
War Diary	Devise	23/11/1917	24/11/1917
War Diary	Villers Faucon	25/11/1917	25/11/1917
War Diary	Devise	26/11/1917	26/11/1917
War Diary	Villers Au Faucon	30/11/1917	30/11/1917
Heading	4th Cavalry Division.Jodhpur Lancers December 1917		
War Diary	Villers Faucon	01/12/1917	01/12/1917
War Diary	W 24.2.0	02/12/1917	03/12/1917

War Diary	Le Mesnil	03/12/1917	17/12/1917
War Diary	Devise	17/12/1917	27/01/1918
Heading	War Diary of 4 Div Troops Jodhpur Lancers For The Month of February 1918		
War Diary	Devise	01/02/1918	06/02/1918
War Diary	Guillacourt	07/02/1918	07/02/1918
War Diary	Oresmaux	08/02/1918	28/02/1918

WO 95/11581

1917-1918
4TH CAVALRY DIVISION (ATTD)

JODHPUR IMP. SERV. LANCERS

~~JAN - DEC 1917~~

JAN 917 to FEB 1918

~~JODHPUR CAV. FLD AMBCE~~

~~JAN - FEB 1918~~

To EGYPT
L of C PALESTINE

SERIAL NO. 172.

Confidential
War Diary
of

JODHPUR IMPERIAL SERVICE LANCERS.

FROM 1st JANUARY 1917 191 **TO** 31st JANUARY 1917 191

WAR DIARY or INTELLIGENCE SUMMARY.

Army Form C. 2118.

(Erase heading not required.)

Hour, Date, Place	Summary of Events and Information	Remarks and references to Appendices
VALINES - S⁺ MARC - BAICOURT FRANLEU 12.7.16	Getting standard lines to front.	
8ᵃ	Advance party of Pioneer Company left with Major to stay at Ht	
9ᵃ - 11ᵃ	The WARLINCOURT	
12 ᵃ	nothing to record	
13ᵃ - 23ᵃ	Remainder of Pioneer Company left with Major at Right "A"	
24ᵃ	nothing to record	
	H 59ᵏᵐ changed billets to FAIREVILLES	
VALINES - S⁺ MARC SAISOURT - FRIREVILLES		
25ᵃ - 27ᵃ	nothing to record	
28ᵃ		
29ᵃ - 31ᵃ	between Hautvin Farm Thi Road half of the camp to Moved against Road half of H⁺ 50 30 - and a little over	

Philip ... Baker

SERIAL No. **172**

Jodhpur Imperial Service Lancers.

1st to 28th February 1917.

Jodhpur Lancers
Army Form C. 2118.

WAR DIARY
or
INTELLIGENCE SUMMARY.

(Erase heading not required.)

Instructions regarding War Diaries and Intelligence Summaries are contained in F.S. Regs., Part II and the Staff Manual respectively. Title pages will be prepared in manuscript.

Hour, Date, Place	Summary of Events and Information	Remarks and references to Appendices
VALINES - SAUCOURT – FRANLEU - ST MARC		
15.2.17.	Major R.J.H. Baddely 15th Lancers joined the regiment.	
17-2-17	Major R.J.H. Baddely " " left regiment for D.H.Q.	
20-2-17	Major P.R. Wheatley 27th Light Cavalry proceeded to join the SIALKOT Rosier Battalion & returned	
	Major P.F. Gell 14th Lancers who rejoined the regiment the same day.	
22-2-17.	Capt. H.F.P. Hornold 5th Cavalry joined the Regiment	
25-2-17.	Lt. Col Holden returned from club in England.	
	as special service officer with H.H. Maharajadhi Perab Singh K.C.I.E etc.	
25.2.17	* 10 Jodian officers proceeded to England on leave	* Party to England consisted of :-
26.2-17	Major A.D.Short D.S.O. 10th Lancers handed over command Rosier Battalion to Major Wheatley & rejoined the Regt.	S. Commander Sultan Singh " " Ram Singh Risaldar Fatal Singh Risaldar Bahadur Singh Risaldar Chatar Sal Singh Jemadar Keshri Singh Jemadar Khem Singh Jemadar Kurwar Singh Jemadar Madan Singh Jemadar Bhopal Singh
		Partap Singh Officer Commanding Jodhpur Lancers

(73989) W4141-463. 400,000. 9/14. H.& J.Ltd. Forms/C. 2118/10.

WAR DIARY
or
INTELLIGENCE SUMMARY.

Army Form C. 2118.

Hour, Date, Place	Summary of Events and Information	Remarks and references to Appendices
1st – 11th VALINES ST. MARC. SAUCOURT FRANLEU	nil.	
12th	Two Officers and 24 other ranks left as a relief to Pioneer Company	
13th	The same number of Officers and men rejoined us from Pioneer Company	
14th – 16th	nil. The whole Pioneer Company rejoined us	
17th	nil	
18th	Marched from VALINES – COULONVILLERS	
19th	" to PERNOIS	
20th	" to ALBERT	
21st	B Echelon x B Echelon was now left at TALMAS	
22nd – 24th	nil B Echelon joined up at ALBERT	
24 25 26	nil Fatigues on roads about PUISIEUX	
26th – 31st	nil	

P. [signature] Belsten
[?] Commanding,
16th (?) S. Lancers.

WAR DIARY

OF

JODHPUR LANCERS

FOR THE
MONTH
OF

APRIL, 1917

Army Form C. 2118.

WAR DIARY
or
INTELLIGENCE SUMMARY.
(Erase heading not required.)

Instructions regarding War Diaries and Intelligence Summaries are contained in F.S. Regs., Part II and the Staff Manual respectively. Title pages will be prepared in manuscript.

Hour, Date, Place	Summary of Events and Information	Remarks and references to Appendices
1st to 5th ALBERT	Nil. Pl	
6th	Marched to Camp S.E. of BIHUCOURT. × Pl	
7th to 9th — BIHUCOURT	Nil weather very snowy. Pl	
10th — — —	Marched to SAPIGNIES & returned to BIHUCOURT Pl	
11th — — —	Marched to MORY & back to BIHUCOURT. This was the day of the 62nd attack on BULLECOURT Pl	
12th — BIHUCOURT	Nil. Pl	
13th — — —	Marched from BIHUCOURT to AVELUY Pl	
14th — — —	Marched from AVELUY to BUS-EN-ARTOIS Pl	
15th to 22nd BUS-EN-ARTOIS	Nil. Pl Corps Commander's inspection of A Squadron horses. Pl	
26th " "	Inspection of rifles by Divisional Armourer. Pl	
25th — 27th — —		
27th — 30th — —	Nil. Pl	

Ralph F Bakewell
Officer Commanding
Jodhpur I.S. Lancers

(73989) W4141—463. 400,000. 9/14. H.&J.Ltd. Forms/C. 2118/10.

No. 5 D.T./4Cav.

Serial No: 142.

WAR DIARY

OF

JODHPUR LANCERS.

For the Month of

May, 1917. + June 1917.

*****

Army Form C. 2118.

WAR DIARY
or
INTELLIGENCE SUMMARY.
(Erase heading not required.)

Instructions regarding War Diaries and Intelligence Summaries are contained in F.S. Regs., Part II. and the Staff Manual respectively. Title pages will be prepared in manuscript.

Hour, Date, Place	Summary of Events and Information	Remarks and references to Appendices
1st BUS EN ARTOIS	Nil P2	
2nd " "	One troop of C. squadron J.L. was detailed as escort to Divisional Commander P2	
3rd " "	Nil P2	
" " "	Inspection of Billets by G.O.C. Lucknow Brigade P2	
4th " "	Nil P2	
5th – 8th " "	Inspection by G.O.C. Lucknow Brigade of horses & equipment P2	
9th " "	Nil P2	
10th – 14th " "	Nil P2	
15th MEAULTE	Marched to MEAULTE P2	
16th "	Marched to SUZANNE P2	
17th SUZANNE	Marched & MESNIL & BRUNTEL P2	
18th–23rd MESNIL LE BRUNTEL	Nil P2	
24th " "	Marched to HAMELET P2	
25th – 28th HAMELET	A few 8" shells dropped round the camp. P2	
30th – 31st "	Nil P2	

Philip Hugh S Bohlen

War Diary
of
Jock Henry Lemon

June, 1917

Army Form C. 2118.

WAR DIARY
or
INTELLIGENCE SUMMARY.
(Erase heading not required.)

Instructions regarding War Diaries and Intelligence Summaries are contained in F.S. Regs., Part II and the Staff Manual respectively. Title pages will be prepared in manuscript.

Hour, Date, Place	Summary of Events and Information	Remarks and references to Appendices
June		
1st–2nd Camp between NAMELET and ROISEL.	Nothing to record.	
3rd — " to 18th — "	Dismounted Company 4 British Officers, 11 Indian Officers, 4 B.O.R., 295 I.O. Rs & 8 followers moved forward to bivouac S.7.S. east of TEMPLEUX & remained there until 9th as an armed Divisional Reserve. They furnished working parties at night for work in the front line during this period. Frequent & violent Thunderstorms. 1 killed by lightning during storm on 11th. Heavy Thunderstorms with big hail storm a few hours broke away & stampeded 4 injured by wire.	8/no 157 & Sown Risoldar Sgt slightly wounded.
19th — "	Dismounted Coy: as above moved from bivouac near TEMPLEUX & took over a piece of front line in Subsector 5, Section B.	
20th — "	Nothing to record.	
21st to 23rd "		
24th — "	Vecenity of Regtl H. Qrs. Camp between HAMELET & ROISEL, Shelled. no damage.	

Army Form C. 2118.

WAR DIARY
or
INTELLIGENCE SUMMARY.
(Erase heading not required.)

Instructions regarding War Diaries and Intelligence Summaries are contained in F.S. Regs., Part II. and the Staff Manual respectively. Title pages will be prepared in manuscript.

Hour, Date, Place	Summary of Events and Information	Remarks and references to Appendices
JUNE 25-6 29th Camp between HAMLET Y RUISEL	Nothing to record.	
30. "	Dismounted Coy; two 1 British officers. 3 I.O. Rs, 1 B.G.R. 71 I.O. Rs & 2 followers who joined Divisional Reserve at HERVILLY, returned from front line reaching Regimental H.Qrs at 4.A.m	

Pratap S Colonel.
Officer Commanding,
Jodhpur I.S. Lancers.

Serial No: **142**
No. 6

WAR DIARY

of

JODHPUR LANCERS.

for the Month

of

July, 1917.

Army Form C. 2118.

WAR DIARY
or
INTELLIGENCE SUMMARY.
(Erase heading not required.)

Instructions regarding War Diaries and Intelligence Summaries are contained in F.S. Regs., Part II and the Staff Manual respectively. Title pages will be prepared in manuscript.

Hour, Date, Place	Summary of Events and Information	Remarks and references to Appendices
1st-4th HAMELET	NIL Pt	
5th — —	Marched to LE MESNIL Pt	
6th-9th LE MESNIL	NIL Pt	
10th "	Horses inspected by the G.O.C. Lucknow Cavalry Brigade Pt	G.O.C. expressed himself very satisfied with the condition of the horses.
11th — 22nd "	NIL Pt	
23rd "	1.3.0.9.5.7. O.Rs 1 Follower sent to Remounts for working party Pt	
24th "	NIL Pt	
25th - 26th "	Divisional Horse Show Pt	3 second prizes, 2 third prizes
26th - 31st "	NIL Pt	

Ralph L.S. Colonel
Officer Commanding
Jodhpur Lancers.

Serial No: 142

WAR DIARY

OF

JODHPUR LANCERS

For

AUGUST, 1917.

Army Form C. 2118.

WAR DIARY
or
INTELLIGENCE SUMMARY.
(Erase heading not required.)

Instructions regarding War Diaries and Intelligence Summaries are contained in F. S. Regs., Part II. and the Staff Manual respectively. Title pages will be prepared in manuscript.

Place	Date August	Hour	Summary of Events and Information	Remarks and references to Appendices
LE MESNIL	1-5th		nil	
	6th		Col. Holden went to Command Reserve dismounted Battalion in the trenches	
	"		Major Riera Singh suffered a shock from lightning	
	7th, 8th		nil	
	9th		Major Gates & Capt. Hornsby went to the Trenches with a dismounted company	
			(I.O. 11. B. & R3. & O R 271)	
	10th		nil	
	11th		I.O. 11. I.O.R. & 1 Follower also juddeed to Meerville in relation to I.O.R.4	
	12th		nil	
	13th		Major Zweil & 1 B. O.R. joined Jodpur Lancers dismounted Company	
			2nd	
	14-17		1/D/224 Buldhem Singh wounded (slight)	
	18		nil	
	19th		J.L. dismounted Coy returned from trenches	
	20th			
	21-31st		nil	

Ramp[?] Colonel
Officer Commanding
Jodhpur I. S. Lancers.

Serial No. 142.

WAR DIARY

OF

JODHPUR LANCERS.

FOR THE MONTH

OF

SEPTEMBER, 1917.

WAR DIARY
or
INTELLIGENCE SUMMARY.
(Erase heading not required.)

Army Form C. 2118

Instructions regarding War Diaries and Intelligence Summaries are contained in F. S. Regs., Part II. and the Staff Manual respectively. Title pages will be prepared in manuscript.

Place	Date	Hour	Summary of Events and Information	Remarks and references to Appendices
LE MESNIL	11th		Nil	
	12th		A hunting party of J.O. & 2 O.R. 7 2 2 went to DIVIS F. to commence building new camp	
	13th		Major Gell went as 2nd in command M. LUCKNOW Bde. to trenches at VADENCURT	
	14th		Nil	
	15th		Captain Hornsby & Lieut Daji Raj special service officers. Indian Photog Sec'n (Commanding - Aman Singh 45 J os & 157 J.O.R. 5" followers on British D.R. went to trenches at VADENCOURT	
	16th		Major Reynolds rejoined Jodhpur Lancers	
			Went to trenches	
	17th		"	
	18th		B.G.C. LUCKNOW Brigade inspected horses of Regiment	
	19th-21st		Nil	
	22nd		Pte Bukta (19163) & Sowar 1037 Janak Singh were slightly wounded	
	23rd		Major Gell returned to horses. 2d Dafa Roy 27 Light Cavalry was killed in action. 1066 Sowar Bahadur Singh was wounded of Lieutenant VERNIER	
	24th		Major W. Heatley S.S.O. joined trench party 3d LE RONIER	
	25th		Nil	
			Major Zind joined the trench party	
	26th		Nil	
	27th-29th		Nil	
	August 30th		The trench party returned to back area LE MESNIL	

Thakur Rajjo Singh
Colonel
Officer Commanding,
Jodhpur I. S. Lancers.

CONFIDENTIAL.

WAR DIARY

OF

JODHPUR LANCERS.

FOR THE MONTH OF

OCTOBER, 1917.

Army Form C. 2118.

WAR DIARY
or
INTELLIGENCE SUMMARY.
(Erase heading not required.)

Instructions regarding War Diaries and Intelligence Summaries are contained in F.S. Regs., Part II and the Staff Manual respectively. Title pages will be prepared in manuscript.

Hour, Date, Place	Summary of Events and Information	Remarks and references to Appendices
1st October 1917 LE MESNIL	Nothing to report	
6.13" "		
14th October	DEVISE - Nothing newly received	
15th Oct to 29 Oct	Nothing to report	
30th Oct	G.O.C. Lucknow Bde inspected newly promoted Indian officers Jemadars Bir Sarup, Gurdhan Singh Bhur Singh Ragmath Singh, Sohan Singh of Alwar Lancers, also Sowar 1296 DITOKAL SINAH, pay shart as recipient of I.O.M. 2nd class (immediate award) for act of gallantry in face of the enemy.	
31st Oct DEVISE	Regiment moved to DEVISE Camp.	

Thakur Pratap Singh
Colonel

No. 4.

(142)

WAR DIARY FOR NOVEMBER, 1917

OF THE

JODHPUR LANCERS.

Army Form C. 2118.

WAR DIARY
or
INTELLIGENCE SUMMARY.
(Erase heading not required.)

Instructions regarding War Diaries and Intelligence Summaries are contained in F.S. Regs., Part II. and the Staff Manual respectively. Title pages will be prepared in manuscript.

Hour, Date, Place	Summary of Events and Information	Remarks and references to Appendices
DEVISE 1.11.17.	nil. Pt	
,, 2.11.17	N.9. O.4 N.C.O went on leave to Paris returning 7.11.17. Pt	X JEM ALIM Khan + R.D
,, 3.11.17	nil Pt	BARISAL SINGH CH
,, 10.11.17.	X 1 BO4 38. O.4 NCO went to 4th Cav Dn Pioneer Bn to MISSY Pt	X Maj Reynolds
,, 11.14 11.17	nil Pt	Risd. Jettesingh
,, 15.11.17	72 men went to MISERY to join 2A Cav Dn Pioneer Bn. Pt	JEM Bahadur Singh
LONGAVESNES 19-11-17	The above dismounted party went to prepare Cavalry track. Pt The Regt marched to LONGASVENES. Pt	JEM. Dh Rulsingh
LEVACQUERIE 20-11-17	Bivouacked notice Hindenburg line N of LE VACQUERIE Pt	
FINS 21.11.17	Returned to FINS. Pt	
,, 22.11.17	Remained at FINS. Pt	
DEVISE 23.11.17	Returned to DEVISE. Pt	
,, 24.11.17	nil. Pt	
VILLERS FAYCON 25.11.17	Regt. to VILLERS FAYCON Pioneer Bn 4th Cav Dn returned to Regt & relieved Pt	
DEVISE 26.11.17	15 DEVISE Pt	
VILLERS FAYCON 30.11.17	nil Pt The Regt marched to VILLERS FAYCON Pt	Ruleep K.S.O Colonel

4th Cavalry Division.

JODHPUR LANCERS

DECEMBER 1917.

WAR DIARY or INTELLIGENCE SUMMARY

Army Form C. 2118.

Jodhpur Lancers

142

Place	Date	Hour	Summary of Events and Information	Remarks and references to Appendices
VILLERS FAUCON	1.12.17	3-30 a.m.	The regiment fell in and orders for a dismounted attack on VILLERS GUISLAIN were issued. Three tanks were to lead the attack. The 30th Jacobs Horse and the Jodhpur Lancers were to supply the first two lines. The 29th in Reserves. The Jodhpur Lancers were to deploy on the left of the road running through X.19 Central. The 36th on the right of the road. The attack to take place at 6-30 a.m. The Brigade moved up to W.24.e.5.8. where it dismounted. Then marched on foot to X.19. Central. Jodhpur Lancers deployed for the attack. No tanks arrived. The dismounted Brigade went with orders to W.24.b. Here some casualties occured from machine gun over shies.	A.
		10-30 a.m.	The Regiment was ordered to support 36th Jacobs Horse who were working along the Railway N of VAUCELETTE FARM. C & D Squadrons moved up to the road running through W.18.B & D. MAJOR TRAIL the Brigade Cavalry was wounded on return from leaving with the 36th who were on the embankment just S of CHAPEL CROSSING. A & B Squadrons following close behind in support Jodhpur Lancers and 36th received orders to consolidate at VAUCELETTE FARM with a view to attacking the BEET FACTORY S of VILLERS GUISLAIN on the VILLERS GUISLAIN road.	A.
		2.20 p.m.	Jodhpur Lancers were ordered to follow the 36th Jacobs Horse. Not to lose touch with the 36th not to lose touch with 36th on the right also on the left. Owing up with the advanced if possible otherwise	A.
		3-45 p.m.	The Jodhpur Lancers were ordered to come up on the left of the 36th on the right also on the left. Owing up with the advanced if possible otherwise to VAUCELETTE FARM. The Jodhpur Lancers advanced from X.19.c.4.4 & reached a line VAUCELETTE FARM to Junction X.13.d.5.1 in touch with Fort Garry Canadian machine guns at the S.E. corner of VAUCELETTE FARM on our left & the head of the 36th on our right. The advance was made under machine gun fire. F.H.E. & Shrapnel. The Gtal casualties on the fm day were as follows:- 1. B. Officer wounded, 1 Indian Officer wounded, 18 Indian Other Ranks wounded, and 5 Indian Other Ranks Killed.	A.
		8-30 p.m.	We were withdrawn to W.24.2.0. in Reserves.	A.

Page 2
Army Form C. 2118.

WAR DIARY *Continued*
or
INTELLIGENCE SUMMARY.
(Erase heading not required.)

Instructions regarding War Diaries and Intelligence Summaries are contained in F. S. Regs., Part II. and the Staff Manual respectively. Title pages will be prepared in manuscript.

Place	Date	Hour	Summary of Events and Information	Remarks and references to Appendices
W24. 2.0	2-12-17		Remained in Reserve.	
LE MESNIL	3-12-17		The Regiment returned to LE MESNIL	
	3rd–5th		Nil	
	6th		Risaldar Keori Singh went on leave to PARIS returning on 12-12-17.	
	7th–12th		Nil	
	13th		Regiment inspected in marching order by G.O.C.	
	14th–16th		Nil	
	17th		Regiment to DEVISE	
DEVISE	17th–25th		Nil	*
	26th		Captain Hornsby & 2 I.O. and 50 I.R. were sent into Camp at –912 Central Trenches the LEVERQUIER Switch.	
	27th–28th		Nil	
	29th		Captain G.N. Pemvick M.O. Jodhpur Lancers was evacuated to Hospital with a broken arm and returned on 31-12-17 afternoon.	
	30th–31st		Nil	

Since 25th a working party of 180, 270 & 83 O.R. have attended daily to LeZX on the corps front.

Maharaj M Khia Singh major
Officer Commanding
Jodhpur I.S. Lancers.

Jodhpur Lancers Army Form C. 2118.

4 Div [Inf?]

WAR DIARY
or
INTELLIGENCE SUMMARY.
(Erase heading not required.)

Hour, Date, Place	Summary of Events and Information	Remarks and references to Appendices
DEVISE 1st January 1918	nil.	
" 2nd "	G.O.C. visited our camp & inspected Hotchkiss Anti Air craft devices.	
" 3rd – 24-1-18	nil.	
" 25th – 1 – 18	Digging party (Squadron Commander PANNAI SINGH & 48 I.O.R.) returned from VENDELLES.	
" 26th 1 – 18	nil.	
" 27th 1 – 18	Lieut Colonel H.N. Holden (to Command Dismounted Brigade.) Major G.R.P. Wheatley, Captain H.F.P. Hornsby, Indian Officers 6 and B.O.R. 3, I.O.R. 113 and Followers 3 went into Reserve in the line at HESBECOURT.	

Pratap Singh Colonel
Officer Commanding
Jodhpur I.S. Lancers.

Serial No. 4

WAR DIARY
OF
JODHPUR LANCERS
FOR THE MONTH OF
FEBRUARY
1918

Army Form C. 2118.

WAR DIARY
or
INTELLIGENCE SUMMARY.
(Erase heading not required.)

Instructions regarding War Diaries and Intelligence Summaries are contained in F. S. Regs., Part II. and the Staff Manual respectively. Title pages will be prepared in manuscript.

Place	Date	Hour	Summary of Events and Information	Remarks and references to Appendices
DEVISE	1st to 4th Feby 18		Nil	
"	5th "	"	Lieut Knight & Jemadar Pitt Singh & 20 O.R.'s went up to the Trenches & relieved Capt Horrex & Jemadar Arjun Singh & 20 O.R.'s who returned to the Camp at DEVISE.	
GUILLACOURT	6th "	"	The Regiment less the numbers in the Trenches, marched from DEVISE camp to GUILLACOURT.	
"	7th "	"	The march was continued from GUILLACOURT. The squadrons were billeted as follows:— A. Squadron at ESTREE-SUR-NOYE. C. Squadron at GRATTEPANCHE. B. Squadron, D. Squadron and Hd. Quarters at ORESMAUX.	
ORESMAUX	8th "	"	Jemadar Gordhan Singh proceeded to England to form part of the Imperial Mounted Escort on the occasion of the opening of Parliament on Tuesday the 12th February 1918 and returned on 23rd February 1918.	
"	9th to 13th	"	Nil.	
"	14th "	"	Lt Colonel Holden, Major Wheatley, Lt Knight & 7 I.O.R., 3 B.O.R., 117 I.O.Rs & 3 Followers returned from the Trenches.	
"	15th to 21st	"	Nil.	
"	22nd "	"	Major Reynolds, 3 I.O.s, 92 I.O.R.s & 3 Followers entrained at SALEUX for TARANTO.	
"	23rd "	"	An additional 10 I.O.Rs entrained at SALEUX for TARANTO.	
"	24th "	"	An additional 3 I.O.S, 1 B.O.R, 19 I.O.R's & 2 Followers entrained at SALEUX for TARANTO.	
"	25th to 26th	"	Nil.	
"	27th "	"	The G.O.C. Division visited the Regiment to bid farewell to the officers proceeding overseas.	
"	28th "	"	Nil.	

Phillip Tury S
Colonel Thakur
Officer Commanding.
Jodhpur I. S. Lancers.
Sirdar Bahadur